Blockchain Simplified

*A Comprehensive Beginner's
Guide to Learn and Understand
Blockchain Technology*

TABLE OF CONTENTS

Introduction

I want to thank you and congratulate you for purchasing the book, *Blockchain Simplified: A Comprehensive Beginner's Guide to Learn and Understand Blockchain Technology.*

This book contains proven steps and strategies on how blockchain technology can be and will be beneficial in the business world. Whether you are a small one man shop or a big billion dollar company, this technology is going to be a necessary addition to your company.

This is because blockchain technology makes it possible for a person or person's to personally be involved with logistical and financial transactions within the company he or she is working for. Blockchain will make it easier to take keep up with all of these transactions by eliminating outside financial auditors.

Unfortunately, the most difficult part of maximizing the effectiveness of blockchain technology in your hands understands just what it is and what it's capable of in the first place. As such, this book will aim to break the core concepts down in such a way that anyone can understand them. First, you will learn the basics of blockchain technology as well as what you can do with them. Next, you will learn how businesses are already taking advantage of this new and disruptive technology.

From there, you will learn about the two primary types of blockchain, those that are based on a proof of work model and those that are based on a proof of stake model and what the differences could mean for you. You will then learn about the many ways you can tell if blockchain technology is right for you right now, and the mistakes to avoid if you do end up deciding to implement your own blockchain for your business. Finally, you will learn about some of the most interesting blockchain projects that are currently on the horizon.

1

Although blockchain is a complicated technology to understand, it is not hard to use. The purpose of this book is to help simplify how this technology works so that you can start using it in your business. You will also learn how other companies have already invested in blockchain and how it has helped these companies improve.

Blockchain technology can also be used by the individual everyday person. As a matter of fact, you have probably already used this technology and didn't even realize it! This technology is the wave of the future being that it is a digitized form of currency type transactions.

Thanks again for purchasing this book, I hope you enjoy it!

Chapter 1

Blockchain Basics

*D*efining *Blockchain Technology:* Whether a person is aware of it or not, he or she conducts business every day, even if that person does not have a job, he is conducting business. How is this possible? Well, it's possible because everyone at some point gets online and initiates in some type of transaction. Whether it be purchasing something from Amazon or simply buying a song off of iTunes, a person has ultimately engaged in the business of blockchain technology.

Even though blockchain technology is a relatively new term, it has actually been around for quite some time. Created by Satoshi Nakamoto, it is a type of digitized ledger or spreadsheet that manages cryptocurrencies and other online trading transactions.

This technology is used in cryptography which is how text is coded on the internet. Cryptography is used in blockchain to create distributed trust networks. This allows any contributor of the network to operate the transactions securely without authorization from someone else in the digital ledger. These transactions are then substantiated, approved and then recorded in an encrypted block. This block is saved intermittently. It is then connected to the previous block which in return creates a chain; making it a blockchain.

There are two main components that make up a blockchain. The first component is a decentralized network. This network facilitates and verifies the transactions that are made. Being on a decentralized network means that the software is not limited to one computer system.

It can be controlled on multiple computer systems. It also means that it is not controlled by the government.

The second component is the indisputable ledger where all transactions are processed and recorded in a secure location. This security makes it extremely impossible for someone not connected to the chain, to make changes or steal information.

There can be many contributors involved in any blockchain. Any of the contributors can control the information being entered into the ledger. Because all transactions are processed securely and given a permanent time-stamp, it becomes very difficult for another contributor to alter the digitized ledger in any way.

This technology can be used for a variety of computerized and internet based applications. One of those is smart-contracts. Smart contracts allow businesses to automatically verify and execute agreements that function independently in a safe and secure environment. Blockchain technology acts as the middleman in executing all business deals, agreements and programmed exchanges of information in smart contracts.

Today's society basically runs online. We rely on the World Wide Web to run not only our personal lives but our business lives as well. With the rise of business being done online, contracts being signed and created online has risen as well.

Blockchain applications have started to become very popular in the medical field as well. Researchers are investigating these applications dealing with digital identity, medical records and insurance records. If you live in a big city, than you have probably already participated in one of these studies. A lot of medical offices now use some kind of digital machine, like a palm scanner, to verify that the information they have on file is in fact your information.

Security concerns: One of the biggest problems people are faced with today is the thought that all their information could be hacked. That is because most all of our information is digitized, and it seems like it has become way too easy to access, copy or tamper with by a complete stranger, yet it is still a risk we all take despite the increasing probability of being hacked. The blockchain technology was created to help make sure that doesn't happen or in the very least make it a lot harder to try.

In order to hack the blockchain system, a person would have to go back and change every single chain. That would require a lot of patience and effort because there could be thousands to billions of blockchains linked that a person would have to go through and change. Changing just one or two will automatically show that the system has been hacked. This is one of the many reasons people are loving this technology!

Blockchain technology can be used for a variety of other things as well. This technology can be and has been used for global payments, music sharing and tracking diamond sales.

Types of blockchains: There are three major types of blockchains. They are public blockchain, private blockchain and consortium blockchain.

Public blockchains are created by the public and anyone can participate in the creation, confirmation and recordation of the content put into the chain. There is not one person in charge of overseeing any transactions that go on in this type of blockchain. Since no one person is in charge of this type of blockchain, decisions are made by many decentralized agreement tools such as proof of work, which is a computer algorithm used by cryptocurrencies (like Bitcoin).

Public blockchains are open and crystal clear in content, so anyone who looks at them will understand what they are and can do. Private blockchains are privately owned by an individual or an organization. These blockchains differ from public blockchains in that there is a designated person in charge. While there can still be several contributors to this type of blockchain, all final transactions are approved/disapproved then recorded by the person in charge.

Consortium blockchains, also known as federated blockchains, the purpose is to remove the only autonomy given to just one contributor by the use of private blockchains. In this type of blockchain, there is more than one contributor in charge. Instead, there are a group of companies or individual people that gather and make decisions that benefit the entire network.

Great Investment: Many companies have already invested in blockchain technology. A poll done in 2016 by Deloitte, showed that companies knowledgeable in this technology had $500 million or more in annual earnings. Researchers polled 308 respondents and twenty-eight percent claimed their company had invested $5 million or more into this technology and ten percent had invested $10 million or more into it.

The same poll showed that forty-two percent of the respondents in the consumer products and manufacturing industry planned to invest more money equaling more than $5 million into blockchain technology. The same with twenty-seven percent of the media and telecoms industry and twenty-three percent of the financial services industry.

Blockchain-based companies: There are already a number of companies that have started just in order to embrace this technology. Let's take a look at some.

Bitcoin is the first blockchain-based technology created. It is a decentralized digital cryptocurrency. This company was also created by Satoshi Nakamoto. Nakamoto is said to have developed the blockchain technology from this company.

Ethereum is an open software system, and it enables a person to build and organize decentralized applications. Through this application, a person can earn ether which can be used to pay for transaction fees and services used on this site.

Augur is a digital betting site. A person can bet on events happening in the real world using blockchain-based currency. Some examples of real world events that can be bet on are athletic sports, winning lottery numbers or how much snow will fall in New York.

Abra is a digital wallet that can be downloaded on your smartphone. It lets you send and receive payments from anywhere in the world. It does not require a person to have a bank account, and there are no transfer fees because it uses its own community of people to handle these transactions.

Blockchain technology is and immutable, encrypted, decentralized ledger that has the potential to make all centralized processes, activities and organizations entirely autonomous. What does this mean in the long run? It means that a person can eliminate the middleman and specialists which will reform every business.

If you found the above confusing don't worry you are probably not the only one. Blockchain technology does not have a great definition that the everyday person can understand. In this chapter, we are going to put things into terms an average person can understand. Let's start with the term itself.

Blockchain technology is simply a way to keep track of any money or trading exchanges you engage in online. It is like your accountant that keeps track of all the money you spend. At the moment it is mostly used to handle any type of situations that deal with cryptocurrency such as Bitcoin.

Example: When you make a transaction using Bitcoin, that transaction is processed through the blockchain. Before the transaction is complete, you or someone connected to your Bitcoin account has to verify that the transaction is legitimate. Once the transaction is verified, it is then recorded and saved to a ledger controlled by blockchain. No one can change or alter the transaction in any way.

Only you or the people who have access to your account can verify transactions.

Blockchain technology is controlled by a decentralized network which means it is not controlled by the government. With today's politics being what they are, it is hard to imagine that there are things they have yet to gain control over. By running on a decentralized network, it is easier to conduct business transactions. It is also more private because you have no federal bank holding your money or other assets. Everything is strictly done by you and your company. To understand how important decentralization is, let's take a look at centralization example and a decentralization example.

Centralization Example

Suppose you use your debit card at the grocery store. You swipe your card to pay for your purchases; then the clerk sends a bill to your bank for the amount agreed to when you paid for your goods. The bank then verifies that it was you who made the purchase. The bank then releases the money to the clerk and then records it to their ledger. The ledger the bank made the recording in includes all transactions the bank has made on behalf of the card used. The bank has complete control over what happens with the ledger. Other than looking at your banking statements online, you have no authority to change anything or do anything to the ledger. Centralized ledgers are also easier to hack into because they are controlled by multiple entities. Decentralization is completely opposite.

Decentralization Example

Imagine you are transferring 1.00 Bitcoin to someone. All you have to do is tell whoever is in charge of the network, whether it be one person or a group of people, that you are transferring 1.00 Bitcoin to so and so. Once completed, the transaction is approved then recorded.

As you can see decentralized blockchains are a lot better because it takes less time to complete one transaction. Other reasons decentralized blockchains are better are that a person or company can send secure information to another person or company, such as medical records and encrypted messages.

Distributed Example

As you can see from the diagram above there is a third type of blockchain network. A distributed network is a network spread across several computing devices that copy and saves the copy to a ledger. It is very much like a blockchain. It is not run by any one entity. Like a blockchain, it can be run be several entities.

Digitized Wallet

A digitized wallet is a piece of software that contains a person's cryptocurrency. This wallet is a person's only record of the cryptocurrency that you own. It is like your real wallet except with invisible money.

Chapter 2

The Business of Blockchain

In this chapter, we are going to discuss how it can be beneficial to add blockchain to your company or daily life if you have not already.

Everyone has trust issues with something in their lives. A lot of people even have mistrust in inputting their information on the internet, but that has not stopped them from doing it. One purpose of blockchain technology is to help ease the distrust people have with inputting their information on the internet. It is one of the main reason's companies are investing their money in using this technology.

A study showed that between 2013 and 2016 blockchain-managed money reached a total of $1.6 billion. That was a 1,600 percent increase. An estimated 1.4 billion in venture capital was put into blockchain startups.

Different Blockchain Industries

The industry that has benefitted a great deal with blockchain is the financial industry. Blockchain has been beneficial in finance because large sums of money and transactions are in play. Here are a couple of examples:

• Crowdlending:

Remember having to go to the bank to get a loan? With Crowdlending you will no longer need to. Crowdlending is a person to person lending company. On average there is more than fifty billion person to person loans worldwide today, and 660 in euros of that was done by Crowdlending in Germany. Blockchain is more than likely to give this field an enormous boost.

• IBM Global Financing Unit:

IBM is one of the major players to use blockchain technology, and the technology has proven to be a great asset for tracing transactions. IBM's Global Financing Unit processes $2.9 million in payables for the company each year, and it is responsible for granting credit to more than four thousand suppliers. IBM has been successful in lowering dispute settlements by twenty-five percent. This decrease in percentage resulted in freeing up $100 million in pre-confirmed capital for other purposes.

Another industry that has benefitted from blockchain technology is bookkeeping. Every transaction that takes place in the economy today is registered internally in the exclusive records of individual market participants. Blockchain technology takes place when accounting expands past the borders of the network.

Adding Value to Your Business

There are many ways in which blockchain technology can add value to a business. One way it adds value is by building a network for your business. Dr. Michael Yuan, Chief Scientist of CyberMiles noted how blockchain can provide value to businesses and startups. His theory is that the "key value blockchain" will deliver the ability to construct a network for all types of businesses. What his theory is stating is that instead of competing against each other, businesses can collaborate and build a network with each business industry having its own chain.

Another way blockchain technology can add value to a business is by "banking the unbanked." Believe it or not, there are a lot of people out there that do not have bank accounts. This technology will allow those people who do not have bank accounts, create one. Someone could simply open a bitcoin account in return having a digital wallet.

The third way this technology can add value to a business is by lowering the transaction time. Again time is playing a major part in the blockchain world. Christopher Brown, CEO of Modular created Blossom. Blossom is noted as a better wallet for Ethereum. This program is a multi-featured desktop wallet application. It gives businesses and users an easier way to handle their funds. It takes less time than if you were to go to the bank to get cash.

The next way value can be added to a business through this technology is through legal contracts. This is done by linking Internet of Things (Io T) data and blockchain technology. Using data from IoT devices allows businesses and individuals to connect to legal contracts that have been saved on the blockchain. For example, suppose you are buying a house. Every document that you sign also has to be signed by the seller; therefore, all the documents need to be in one place for both the seller and the buyer to have access to. Outside information from IoT connected devices is linked to the blockchain, making all of the legal contracts usable immediately without anyone else interfering in the process.

The final way in which blockchain technology can add value to the business is by helping with monetization. The ways of making money for businesses is changing in today's society. People no longer pay attention to ads because on television they can fast forward through them and online they can ignore them plus the money generally goes to the site where the ad is placed.

This has had a big impact on businesses.

That is why blockchain is important in adding value regarding monetization because it solves the problem. It solves the problem because every part of the content created for ads is recorded on the blockchain which is how content creators are rewarded through cryptocurrency or fiat currency (a government legalized currency, but it is not backed by a commodity.)

Way of the Future

Many experts believe blockchain technology is the wave of the future, and what follows is a number of compelling reasons why this may be the case

Growing Money

Cryptocurrency is vastly growing due to the fact that people want to put their money somewhere it will not only be safe and secure, but it will also gain value just it would if it were in a savings account. Savings accounts, however, are not as secure as a society would like then to be. In late 2017, future markets had already been created for the cryptocurrency site Bitcoin. The year 2017, was also the year the finance industry saw an increase in Initial Coin Offerings (ICO). ICO's gained more money than venture capital investments.

While cryptocurrencies continue to progress in their abilities to process transactions faster, they will eventually compete against credit card companies processing of transactions.

Blockchain & The Cloud

Everyone has at some point used the cloud to back-up data they do not want to lose. The cloud can runs on a blockchain. Experts say that people take this luxury for granted. In the old days, you couldn't just click a button and automatically save data to a backup site like iCloud and Dropbox, you actually had to take and place in a compact disk or flash drive. Then insert the disk or flash drive to another computer to download the data.

While people still can do this today, there is no guarantee that this type of technology will last. Like floppy disks, compact disks and flash drives could one day be obsolete, but internet based saving applications will always be updated. That is because we live in a tech savvy world.

Who Wants to Play Games?

The gaming world of eSports and online fantasy sports has grown over the past decade with people creating online fantasy teams. Online games, like Fantasy Football, were some of the first sites to adopt the earliest versions of cryptocurrencies and use blockchain to run and keep up with the gaming technology.

It was noted that the fantasy sports industry is worth $7 billion or more. FanDuel and DraftKings own ninety percent of the fantasy sports industry and companies like MyDFS already allow users to create virtual lineups of real players and receive winnings by earning tokens. The winnings are based on a player's performance and their bet on the performance of other competing players and more.

It doesn't just stop with fantasy sports. The most popular smartphone applications to download are games. That's why as this technology grows, it will become more likely that other developers in the online gaming world will make use of it along with cryptocurrencies.

Additional uses

There are several more useful things that blockchain technology can do. The first deals with supply chain management. Blockchain benefits supply chain management by being able to trace goods while being cost effective.

An example of this is sending a package through the United Parcel Service from one business to another. In the old days, a person had to call to find out where their package if hadn't arrived when it was supposed to, but now you are sent a tracking number straight to your email. Through this tracking number, you can tell where the package you sent or are waiting for is in transit which creates a blockchain.

This wonderful technology makes it easier for businesses to do business together because it has simplified the transfer process, production process, verification and payment method used from business to business.

The second benefit of using this technology is quality assurance. Let's be honest, mistakes happen in business and it is not always easy to pin down how this mistake or error occurred. With a blockchain, errors can be traced back to the point of origin in which the error was made. This not only makes it easier to investigate errors made, but it also saves time and money. It also makes it easier to perform the necessary actions to make the error right.

A good example of this is the 2018 e coli roman lettuce outbreaks. When it was reported that traces of e coli had been found in Roman Lettuce, suppliers were able to trace back to the date the contamination occurred, and it was promptly reported to the public.

Another benefit of blockchain technology is in voting. Voting requires a level of trust in that the votes aren't rigged in some way. Blockchain technology is currently being tested in some places to decrease the chance of voting fraud from occurring.

A good example of this is when NASDAQ influenced blockchain technology to help shareholder voting. They did it by joining forces with their blockchain partners and the local digital identification solutions which had provided government officials with their identity cards. The project was successful.

Smart contracts

Smart contracts run on a variation of the original blockchain code that is broadly referred to as blockchain 2.0, in addition to offering enhancement when it comes to scalability and transaction speeds, it allows for the use of more complicated code to be compiled into a given block. This feature has given rise to the smart contract. A smart contract is simply a piece of computer code that can be activated once certain conditions are met as determined by the blockchain as a whole. The smart contract can then do things like transfer funds between individuals or make a trade once these conditions have been met.

Smart contracts utilize applications created on the platform they are a part of to do things like contract facilitation and negotiation. The benefits of these contracts are that the blockchain makes it easy to enforce and verify them, though they are not, in the strictest sense, enforceable under the law like traditional contracts. Their decentralized nature also makes it very difficult to censor them or instigate any type of fraud while using them as they are based on binary conditions that anyone with access to the blockchain can easily confirm.

When it comes to dealing with the legalese that fills most traditional contracts, it can be difficult for those without a law degree to make heads or tails out of who owes what to whom and how these clauses will come into effect. Smart contracts have the potential to cut through this legal red tape in a big way by automating parts of the process based on communal blockchains. They can ensure that x happens only if y happens first and is verified through the appropriate third party. There would be no need for this boilerplate type of content simply because it will all be handled automatically.

Besides just making the process more efficient, and simpler all around, smart contracts will also have the benefit of ensuring that everyone with access to a given contract can easily determine if a given event has taken place as well as when the event took place. There will be no room for disagreement as everything that occurs will be clearly outlined in block form and timestamped besides. Certain contracts will never take this step, however, specifically those that are required to uphold a great degree of secrecy.

Blockchain technology is constructed in such a way that it could conceivably be used to replace traditional notary services. There are already numerous different apps available that allow for notarization of a variety of different types of content. Smart contracts also have the possibility to reinvent insurance in a big way. Rather than deal with insurance agents who have to determine liability in case of a business-related injury, a blockchain would be able to make use of a smart contract that issues payments if a specific interconnected item registers a faulty signal. Blockchain would then allow for a more streamlined claim process that would improve the customer experience and ultimately save the company money.

Smart contracts could even be used to save lives! Real world tests are already being done that links individuals to their healthcare status as they are going through a hospital. Early studies show that this practice can decrease errors by up to 30 percent in nonemergency situations. This is a huge step forward for hospitals that are often not designed for the volume and range of data that is being created these days. Patient data can even continue to be gathered on an outpatient basis or if the individual has agreed to be part of a test group. Payment for these tests could then be issued automatically once the required data has been successfully gathered.

Chapter 3

Proof of Work Versus Proof of Stake

As already mentioned, a majority of the public blockchains that are currently available are based on a proof of work system. However, throughout 2018, Ethereum, the second biggest cryptocurrency in the world, has been testing out a new system that would switch its blockchain from a proof of work to a proof of stake system. Just what that means will be explained soon, but first, it is important that you understand just what is occurring when a transaction is verified. As Bitcoin is the largest proof of work blockchain in the world, a comparison of the two should make the benefits and drawbacks of each system clear.

Proof of Work

Bitcoin mining is accomplished by using a high-powered machine that will utilize a SHA256 double round hash verification process with the purpose of validating bitcoin transactions as they occur in order to provide security for the sanctity of the bitcoin blockchain. The speed at which your machine is able to mine bitcoins is measured in terms of hashes per second.

In exchange for this service, bitcoin compensates its miners by offering up a fraction of a bitcoin per validation in order to offset energy and time costs. Additionally, those who initiate the transaction typically provide some amount of transaction fee to help offset costs as well. The greater the computer processing power of your bitcoin mining machine the more you stand to make through this process.

The reason that this is required is that in order to be accepted into the blockchain, each block must have a valid proof of work. A proof of work is a type of data that is both time consuming and difficult to produce. Producing a proof of work is essentially a random process with low probability of success which means that a bitcoin mining machine trying to complete the process requires a great degree of trial and error in order to find success. Bitcoin uses what is known as the hashcash proof of work.

The hashcash proof of work is a type of cryptographic algorithm which makes use of a hash function as a core building block of the process. The most common hashcash function used these days is hascash-Sha256. This proof of work function was created back in the 1990s by Dr. Adam Back and was originally used as a way of preventing email spam abuse as successfully generating the hashcash for a single email is simple but creating one for a vast number of emails all at once (as spammers are wont to do) was much more difficult.

Hashcash proofs of work can be tweaked for difficulty in order to ensure that new blocks are not generated faster than the network can handle which means a new block cannot currently be generated more than once every 10 minutes. As the probability of each successful generation is quite low, this makes it difficult to determine which bitcoin machine is going to generate the next block.

In order for a new block to be considered valid, its hash value must end up being less than that of the current target which means that each block then naturally indicates that work has been done to generate it. Each block also contains the hash of the preceding block which is how the chain as a whole understands where each block falls into the overall blockchain. As such, changing a block can only be accomplished by redoing the work on all the previous blocks and generating new and connected hashes for all of them. As the computational power for such a task would be enormous, this essentially protects the blockchain from tampering.

Proof of Stake

While most of the major cryptocurrencies out there work off some variation of the proof of work model, either through the SHA256 hash or though another, similar hash, Bitcoin's biggest competitor Ethereum has been working on an alternative that could dramatically change the way blockchain transactions are verified in the future.

In May 2017, the platform released the implementation guide for a hybrid proof of work/proof of stake system that is being rolled out in phases to test the new system before it becomes the blockchain's primary verification system. The current plan states that the blockchain will alternate between the two systems in such a way that one out of every 100 blocks will use the new system while the rest will continue using the old for the time being.

The hope is that the new system will improve the rate at which new blocks can be produced, which marks the first step in the plans for Ethereum's evolution. When the system goes wide it will mark the first time a proof of stake system has been used to secure a blockchain, which will be a major step forward, despite the modest initial rollout. It will serve as the proof of concept test for an alternate to the proof of work model that has dominated the early days of cryptocurrency development and thus provide proponents a chance to finally test their claims of its superiority. One thing that is already known for sure is the fact that when it is eventually rolled out on a larger scale the proof of stake model will reduce the amount of electricity required to verify a block significantly.

To understand why this change could be so huge for Ethereum, it is important to understand just how it differs from the proof of work model. With a proof of stake verification system, instead of having the miner solve the equation in order to verify the block, a validator, who is confirmed reliable by the stake they have in the system, will commit to its accuracy, knowing that if they lie they will lose their own ether as well. The Alliance is currently testing the new system through a limited use verification process to make sure it is ready for a wider launch next year.

During the first stage of deployment, all of the blocks that are verified through the new system will also be verified through the old system as well. This will help to double verify the blocks contain the information that they should while also testing the accuracy of the new system at the same time. It will also mark the first time the new fork rules will come into play that users have an actual choice about. Validators will then look at the various chains that are available and then make a decision based partially on how much ether is currently in the chain. If they choose poorly, they will then lose money. This process with then form a consensus that leads to a single larger chain from many smaller ones.

The completed smart contract with then be added to the blockchain proper where it will form what will be known as a Casper account that anyone who is interested in becoming a validator can sign up for. They will then need to deposit a set amount into the system in order to keep them honest. With this done, they will then be able to take part in the new virtual mining process.

Assuming the initial stage goes smoothly, the second phase will involve deployment on a much larger scale. What's more, it will involve the creation of a difficulty timebomb which is essentially a bit of malicious code that will serve to make mining Ethereum via a proof of work model more and more difficult over time. The idea here is that these difficulty spikes will cause miners to feel as though mining in the traditional way is ineffective compared to the new system that's already up and running. Eventually, the theory goes, things will get so bad under the old system that even the most diehard of holdouts will have no choice but to switch to the new process.

This doesn't mean the transition is going to be without issue, however, starting with the fact that it has the potential to cause a hard fork in the cryptocurrency as opposed to a soft one. If this is the case, and enough people to switch to the proof of stake system then they could decide to go on with the Ethereum blockchain before the timebomb was created and thus create a third type of Ethereum besides Ethereum Classic and regular Ethereum. As Ethereum Classic was only created after a similar fork occurred, it certainly remains a possibility.

While it might not be all smooth sailing, this doesn't mean that the proof of stake model is going to lose out. After all, it contains a number of clear benefits over the more traditional process, starting with the fact that it would drop the more than 1 million dollars Ethereum miners are spending on electricity each day do to about 10 percent of that.

What's more, in addition to making it cheaper, the proof of stake model will also make mining more egalitarian as it won't matter how fast the user's computer is because all the actual calculation will be done within the blockchain itself. As an added bonuses, this makes the 51 percent attack much more difficult to pull off successfully. A 51 percent attack occurs when a group of miners band together to control more than 51 percent of all nodes running a particular blockchain in an effort to add completely false blocks to the system that the no affected nodes will then accept as true because a majority of the nodes are already reporting it that way.

It will also take things even another step further still by making it possible to ensure validators stay honest by forcing them to be vested in the transactions they verify as they know if they don't play fair they will lose the money they put into the system in order to start validating in the first place. Finally, it makes it easier to produce blocks faster than ever thanks to a process known as sharding. All told, the proof of stake model naturally increases scalability across the board as it makes the process less complicated when it comes to determining the authenticity of each block as all it will require is knowing who had the greatest stake and who had the most hashing power.

Sharding is the name given to the process of breaking a larger database down into more manageable pieces or shards. This allows each shard to have its own set of validators who then complete their own transactions within the shard. Once sharding occurs, it will then make scalability more modular and thus even faster. This is in comparison to the proof of work model wherein there is a finite limit to the number of miners who are working on a proof at a given time. By instead separating all of the validators into different shards, you allow them all to work on different problems at the same time, increasing the overall speed of the system as a whole significantly.

This won't be all good news, however, as the process isn't without its share of issues as well. First among them is the fact that the new system is not guaranteed to work as a proof of stake model has never been put into play at this scale before. This means that there is a possibility that the primary blockchain could be harmed if the transactions aren't processed as planned or if a smart contract is written incorrectly. To combat this possibility, the Ethereum team is working hard on what is being called the finality property which is going to ensure that the current state of the blockchain is secure before the new one can be brought online.

Chapter 4

Deciding if Blockchain Technology
is Right for You

If you like what you have heard so far, then you are likely interested in experimenting a little with blockchain as a way of determining if it is the right course of action for you and your company. The most common reasons that people typically consider experimenting with blockchain is an ongoing desire to experiment with new technologies, a need for blockchain's timestamp technology or an interest in the many ways blockchain can safeguard existing data. It is important to look before you leap, however, and consider the following to see if blockchain is really for you.

Know who is going to be looking at your data: In most traditional centralized databases, anyone with access to the database has their activities stored in case they need to be reviewed later. If you have a need for many individuals to look at your data on a regular basis, but don't actually want to give any of them write access then a blockchain may streamline this process by providing read only access in addition to a log in a more traditional sense when required.

Writeable data: Your average user database is typically protected via a mix of usernames and passwords along with several levels of restricted access. Even more security measures can then be implemented to prevent high-level data from being accessed when it shouldn't. All of this is still less than the standard blockchain security protocols which always makes it perfectly clear who created which blocks and the time and place they did so.

This ensures that each transaction is always completed with the full knowledge of the creator who can then confirm and sign off on the transaction assuming the individuals are not adding information directly from a node. This signature is then further confirmed before the block is added to the chain. Even if a username and password combination is not required in order for users to have access (not recommended) the chain will still automatically log the IP address of any user who creates new blocks.

Data alteration: If you are planning on altering the data that you are going to store in the blockchain, then you may want to rethink your plans. With a centralized database, altering data is as simple as tracking down the appropriate clearance, changing the required data and having those changes saved in a log. By contrast, the only way to do the same with data that has already been stored in a blockchain is to simultaneously change it across 51 percent of the nodes that are available on the network. While this is certainly a useful security feature in some scenarios, it also automatically disqualifies blockchain databases from the running in several others.

Data restoration: If you find yourself spending a serious amount of time doing nothing but updating backup data, then you might find blockchain technology to be extremely useful. If you are using a traditional database then you are going to have to instigate backups manually and will have to worry about making sure everything is where it needs to be yourself. On the other hand, when it comes to a distributed database, the information is automatically updated across all available nodes, every time new information is added to the blockchain. As such, as long as all of your nodes don't fail catastrophically all at the same time, then you have nothing to worry about. What's more, depending on the costs that are ultimately associated with backing up and updating all of your data, you may actually find that the additional operation costs that are going to come along with a decentralized database may actually make it the cheaper of the two alternatives.

Easy to share: While centralized databases are often extremely limited in terms of access, a blockchain database can easily be temporarily connected to another blockchain database, making the process of transferring information between the two extremely painless. These other blockchains could be related to specific departments within your company, or even related to complete different companies. If you are considering taking this step, it is important to keep in mind that when you give someone access to your blockchain, you are giving them access to your entire blockchain, nothing is off limits. This may require significant planning in order to utilize effectively if you deal with a lot of sensitive data.

Storage limitations: One area where a traditional database has a blockchain database beat is in the amount of data that can be comfortably stored. When a new node is created for a decentralized database, the entirety of the blockchain is downloaded to it. This, coupled with the fact that nodes can be thousands and thousands of miles apart from one another means that it is in your best interest to keep the total amount of data in your blockchain as manageable as possible. As a general point of reference, the Bitcoin database has only about 100 gigabytes and it has been around for nearly a decade. If you are looking for a high capacity option, then looking elsewhere might be a better choice.

Verification process: Assuming you are planning on running a private blockchain then you don't need to worry about paying a reward for the validation of blocks, in fact, you don't need to worry about a proof of work model at all. Instead, you are going to want to use a proof of stake model, as everyone in the private blockchain is going to have a stake in keeping in up to date and reliable which means the process for validating can be much more straight forward. Even still, you are going to need to factor in the amount of time that this process will require and ensure that you have the manpower to facilitate it.

The next step

After looking over the specifics, assuming you decide that taking advantage of blockchain technology makes sense for you, it is important to consider exactly what you plan on using the technology for. If you are an existing business owner who hopes to get in ahead of the curve on the next big thing, then you will want to focus on the many potential ways blockchain and smart contract technology can work together to improve many of the ancillary aspects of your business. Specifically, you are going to want to take a long hard look at things that have the potential to decrease costs or improve efficiency.

This means you will also need to consider all the many ways that utilizing a blockchain will make you more competitive in the eyes of the competition by allowing you to get the jump on the emerging trends in your industry. Alternately, you will want to consider the various disruptions to the way your business works that blockchain might bring to light, and work to move things around now, so the disruption is as minimal as possible. Remember, being aware of what is likely coming next will make it easier to face head on.

If you are looking to form a new business based around blockchain technology, then the best way to get started is to work with as many different blockchains as possible. This will not only help to improve your grasp of the technology but will also help to make the technology more mainstream, which is what is needed in order for new blockchain companies to really takeoff. If you ever hope to break into the mainstream via blockchain, then you are going to want to do everything in your power to ensure blockchain becomes as mainstream as possible.

It is important to keep in mind that it is likely going to be a tough road to hoe, however, as many of blockchain's greatest benefits are only going to be available to companies who already have the existing infrastructure to take advantage of them as fully as possible. As such, the most realistic forecast for the rise of blockchain technology is that there will be a handful of new companies that are going to come along and grab a share of the spotlight, while the rest of the room at the top is taken up by the members of the old guard who are able to get their acts together and make a move on blockchain technology before their competition has a chance to.

This is not a knock on blockchain technology, this is simply the way new technology is often assimilated into the mainstream. Remember, understanding this tendency is the best way to circumvent it and find the success you seek.

Chapter 5

Blockchain Implementation
Mistakes to Avoid

With all of the hype that blockchain systems have been generating in both financial and technical sectors, it can make it easy to leap without looking in terms of implementing your own blockchain distributed system. This is a folly, however, and before you take the plunge you should make sure you are avoiding all of the mistakes listed below, just in case.

Not having realistic expectations: If you are planning on ever using a blockchain efficiently, the first thing you have to understand is that it is not a catchall solution to every problem. Luckily, as long as you set up a private system, only a few people will ever have to know if the initial testing ends up going poorly.

This also goes for the amount of information that is routinely stored in each block. Remember, the bulk of the entire blockchain is going to be ultimately duplicated to each new node that is created, so an extremely bloated chain is going to be adding unnecessary bloat to all of the computers using it. Keep in mind, the entire Bitcoin blockchain is only 55 gigs. While it is great when it comes to securely store private databases, it is not the best choice when it comes to large scale data usage, in those cases a centralized data storage system is actually the better choice.

Likewise, it is important that while blockchain systems and smart contracts, in particular, have numerous fail safes in place to prevent user error, that doesn't mean it is infallible. The very fact that each block is only referred to by a hash key makes it much more likely for humans to mistake blocks for other blocks to everyone's detriment. Be sure to implement a failsafe to check this sort of thing for the best results.

Underestimating the time required to fully understand the intricacies of blockchain technology: If you plan on seeing the implementation of a blockchain system through to completion, it is important to understand exactly how much time is required to learn to utilize it to its fullest potential. What's more, while picking up this book and reading through it is a good first step, it is only that, which means you are likely going to need to do more research to understand the best way to implement a blockchain that best serves your purposes. This means you will want to understand what you are going to be using it for on a regular basis but also what any secondary or even tertiary duties might be.

Only after you have a clear idea of just what you are going to be ultimately going to be using the blockchain system for will you be able to determine which type of creation software of the many available is going to be right for you and your needs. While not yet mainstream, that doesn't mean that the market for blockchain creation tools is not already crowded which means that knowing exactly what you are looking for is the first step to finding it reliably and effectively. Choosing poorly at this step can make the blockchain creation process much more difficult than it ultimately needs to be which is why doing your research and not becoming overeager is so important.

Not being patient: After you have a clear idea of just what the uses for your blockchain distributed database is going to be and how you are likely going to go about implementing the blockchain it is important to not be in a hurry to finish and to instead take things at a more measured pace. The process for setting up your own blockchain, as discussed in chapter 5, can be long and complicated but it is important to follow it through to the letter as well as testing your blockchain fully before beginning to rely on it in a real world setting. Remember, setting up a good blockchain takes time and rushing it is only going to cause you problems, in the long run, every single time.

With this in mind, it is important that you decide on a time table that accurately reflects how long the project is going to take you from start. When working out this time table it is important to consider the time it will take to get buy-in from anyone else whose opinion is required before anything can get started. This process will likely go much more smoothly if you have already followed through on the above suggestions in such a way that it is clear why a blockchain database is the right choice and how it will go from being an idea to being a reality.

Not limiting access: When it comes to an exciting new technology like blockchain, it is perfectly natural for a large number of individuals to be interested in testing it out for themselves. If your blockchain is private, then it is important to not let too many people have access until they have been trained properly. A few inexperienced hands at the helm can easily derail a fledgling blockchain that doesn't yet have the internal infrastructure to self-correct under a deluge of inaccurate information. When it comes to accessing the core of the blockchain in a private system it is important to store the key for private access that is generated with a new blockchain in a safe location as if it is lost there is no way to regain control of the blockchain.

Not understanding how smart contracts and regular contracts differ: Despite the name, it turns out that smart contracts and actual contracts have relatively little directly in common. Nevertheless, the technology is so new that it is easy for misinformation to spread without an easy counter of the truth readily available to deploy in response. First and foremost, it is important to understand that smart contracts are not, in fact, a legally binding agreement in a traditional sense. Instead, they are actually a type of process that can be automated and set to trigger when certain binary factors are met. As an example, you could utilize a smart contract to ensure your car payment is made each month until the balance owed is zero. That same smart contract is not, however, in anyway legally binding when it comes to forcing you to make a payment each month.

They can, however, be used as part of a legally binding agreement, so that they take care of the specifics of the if/then nature of most binding contracts. For example, with a legally binding contract saying it is acceptable, a smart contract could be used to cut the power to the battery of your car so that you can't use it until you make your monthly payment.

While smart contracts are not legally binding, they are also different than Ricardian contracts as well. A Ricardian contract can be thought of as a way of legally determining liability and while smart contracts can be told to activate only after multiple instances of liability have been obtained then still can't obligate anyone to do anything. Smart contracts don't consider liability; they either are activated or they aren't there is no middle ground.

Additionally, it is important to keep in mind that while they can be programed to do a wide variety of different things and to keep an eye out for numerous variables, smart contracts are little more than binary processes that then go on to trigger specific outcomes when trigger. They are driven solely by external events which inherently limits what they can be successfully used for. What those limits are is decreasing, however, which is why the number of possible uses that it has moving forward can be quite significant.

This usage case scenario list will continue to grow and as it does, the number of people who become comfortable using blockchains increase, which will, in turn, cause the potential uses from the technology to grow even more. While they have a limited number of potential functions, the variety of uses for those functions is staggering which means that any routine action that has clear distinguishing factors regard success or failure has the potential to be operated via blockchain and smart contract as long as there are an internet connection present and a list of transactions telling it what to do.

Finally, it is important to keep in mind that that a smart contract can take up an individual block in a blockchain but the two are very different things, even if they are occasionally used interchangeably. If you have a hard time keeping them separate in your mind, simply remember that a blockchain contains all of the information and a smart contract uses the other information in the blockchain to activate when appropriate. Furthermore, a blockchain is a distributed database, while a smart contract is an instance of distributed computing instead.

Chapter 6

Blockchain Projects of Note

For quite some time, blockchain projects of all shapes and sizes were perceived by those in the know as little more than a feckless gamble. Admittedly this is with good reason as the industry as a whole was still in its absolute infancy making it difficult to determine where anything would end up and how it would all shake out. While blockchain technology is still not anywhere near the mainstream, more than a billion dollars has been invested so far and some of those investments are starting to pay off in a major way.

While most blockchains are currently confined to the financial sector, that is not where they are going to stay for long and developers and investors from around the world are already considering new ways that its unique benefits can be put to use. Regardless of their individual success, it is safe to say that blockchain technology has serious infrastructure implications when it comes to things like identity protection, intellectual property, energy, supply chain management, bureaucratic red tape and more. The rest of this chapter includes a variety of projects that are worth keeping an eye on.

Hyperledger: While not technically an entirely new project, Hyperledger is a concentrated opensource effort to create new ways to make it possible for developers to bring together multiple separate blockchains in a way that will allow them to communicate with one another directly. This collaboration spans the globe and is currently sponsored by the Linux Foundation in addition to serious players in the supply chain, technology, manufacturing, finance, Internet of Things and banking sectors.

Essentially, what this means is that the next level of implementation when it comes to blockchain technology is likely going to be what really propels future blockchain projects and applications into the mainstream. A vast majority of the success of this project is going to be based on the success the developer community receives both individually and as a whole as well as the contributions it receives from well-established businesses that are legitimately committed to its success. Due to its opensource nature, anyone with the talent, inclination or cash to get involved is encouraged to contact the Linux Foundation for details on how they can get involved.

Blockstream: Blockstream is a company that is dedicated to the idea of the blockchain future, so much so that they have several interesting projects in the works at the same time. Perhaps the most innovative of them all is one that involves fueling the acceleration of cryptocurrency-based projects in tandem with open asset and smart contract technologies. Another worthwhile project to watch is their Liquid project which is already being used to increase the transfer speeds of multiple bitcoin exchanges.

The company attracted more than 55 million dollars in its series A funding which is being put to work in an effort to enhance the strength of its security protocol and bring additional smaller projects online as well. One such project is the Lightning Network which can be thought of as a speed boost to smaller blockchain transactions. It operates a second sidechain that is attached to a primary and it only accepts transactions up to a certain size. This not only ensures these smaller transactions can be completed more quickly as they don't get stuck in line behind massive transactions, it also ensures large transactions are processed as quickly as possible as none of the primary blockchain's resources will end up going towards these smaller transactions.

Lisk: Generally speaking, Lisk has a number of similarities to Ethereum, though there are some crucial differences as well. For one, Lisk was created based on JavaScript and, more importantly, it is primarily designed to work with sidechains instead of actual blockchains. Its primary goal is to make it as easy as possible for the average user to code and deploy their own decentralized applications. The company managed to raise more than six million dollars during its initial funding round which was enough to ensure they were able to start work on a host of additional features and services.

As the existing blockchain infrastructure and programming requires can be quite arcane, one of Lisk's best features is its simplicity in that it was designed from the ground up to be as simple and as intuitive as possible. What's more, they must be doing something right as the company is currently working directly with Microsoft to add their platform to the Azure cloud and to integrate it into the Azure blockchain as well.

Ripple: The goal of Ripple is nothing less than the complete revolutionization of the dominant financial structures at play today. As if that wasn't enough, they are also working to create what they call the Internet of Value. They believe that the current system that's in place to support international payment is in need of a serious makeover as it is not nearly adequate enough to keep pace with the needs of the worldwide community which means it is falling further and further behind user expectations. The company is already working with numerous banks around the world in an effort to bring new blockchain-based technologies to a wider financial audience and transform the way money is sent and received around the world.

Specifically, their system works to make it easier for banks to send payments between disparate systems in real time across an extremely secure network that also makes it easier for those with the need to access settlements that are exclusively bank-based. It also prioritizes real-time traceability, lowered costs and increasing the overall speed at which funds of this type are sent.

Aeternity: The Aeternity company is actively working on the development of solutions that make it easier for the Ethereum blockchain to scale depending on the needs of the network at the

36

moment, thus dramatically increasing transaction speeds as a result. The company is also working to create a network that is capable of handling every transaction and smart contract in a state channel to ensure that the number of total transactions that the blockchain is capable of handling increases dramatically. When it is online, it will shunt most of the processing power required for monitoring smart contracts to a sidechain that will only need to bother the main chain when it is created, when it activates and if anything goes awry in the interim.

Dfinity: The Dfinity project is creating an entirely new blockchain as the basis for creating a brand-new form of artificial intelligence it is calling the Blockchain Nervous System which will serve to curtail many of the issues that other blockchains have had when it comes to accurately guiding the network as effectively as possible. It will work by essentially choosing a market direction at random to which users will either react negatively or positively. The AI will then learn from these responses and work to determine the best new tactic to facilitate the overall growth and longevity of the market. It also aims to solve most common scalability issues by storing key data in shards that are then spread out across the network.

ContentKid: This disruptive payment company is already making use of blockchain technology in hopes of providing users access to short-term subscriptions to a wide variety of different types of content that would otherwise be gated behind a more traditional subscription. As such, if you were so inclined you could set up a ContentKid account and watch the final season of Game of Thrones once it has finished airing all at once as opposed to paying for several months of an HBO subscription. As you watch funds would be automatically deducted from your account seamlessly. The solution comes from using the HyperLedger blockchain which ensures that users can access premium content without the fear of fraud or resorting to illegal options.

Blockphase: This blockchain-based tool is used to enforce copyright claims for creators of virtual reality, augmented reality or 360-degree video content. Users can upload their content to the Blockphase platform which then allows the company to automatically monitor the whole of the internet for instances of content being used without permission. Making it possible for users to store and manage their copyrights on a blockchain network also makes it possible for them to decrease their overall risk of fraud, making it easier for them to focus more on creating content and less on ensuring no one steals it.

Chain of Things: The Chain of Things works to combine two disruptive technologies in hopes of solving serious issues facing the world today. Specifically, it is working to create a link between the Internet of Things and blockchain technology as a whole with the goal of reducing fraud and thus increasing efficiency as a result.

Flowchain: Flowchain is a distributed ledger that works with the Internet of Things to make it possible for devices to access relevant information as it occurs. It is a peer-to-peer networking system that offers faster information transfer speeds compared to the current way these devices can communicate with one another. The application of this distributed ledger includes things like connecting smart cars and even entire cities over the Internet of Things, all to one interconnect blockchain infrastructure.

Conclusion

Thank you for making it through to the end of *Blockchain Simplified: A Comprehensive Beginner's Guide to Learn and Understand Blockchain Technology*, let's hope it was informative and able to provide you with all of the tools you need to achieve your goals, whatever it is that they may be. Just because you've finished this book doesn't mean there is nothing left to learn on the topic, expanding your horizons is the only way to find the mastery you seek.

Furthermore, as what the technology is capable of as well as who the major players in the scene are is still being determined, it is likely that there was a new blockchain breakthrough while you were reading this book. As such, the only way you can ever truly hope to master blockchain technology is if you dedicate yourself to becoming a lifelong learner in the space. After all, learning about blockchain technology is a marathon, not a sprint which means that slow and steady win the race.

Finally, if you found this book useful in any way, a review on Amazon is always appreciated!

www.ingramcontent.com/pod-product-compliance
Lightning Source LLC
Chambersburg PA
CBHW071152220526
45468CB00003B/1028